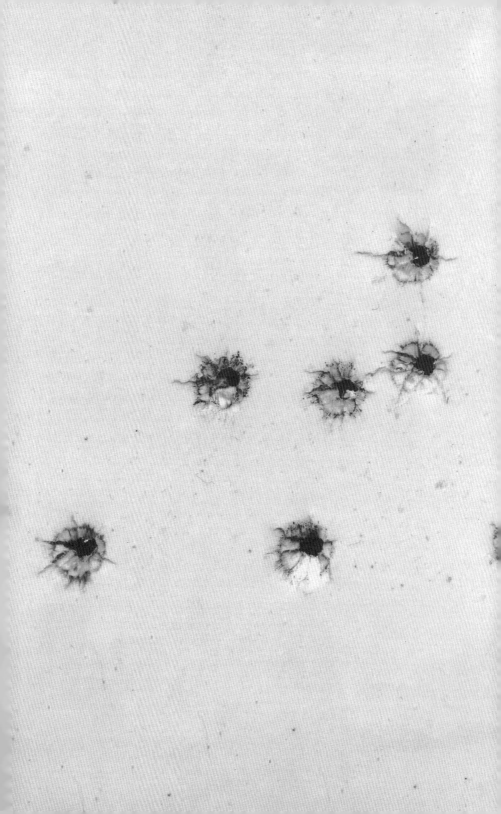

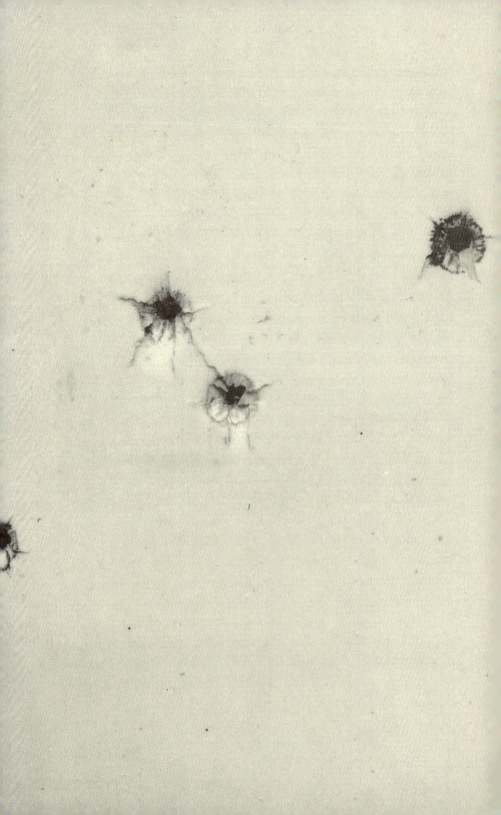

THIS IS A STICKUP

ALSO BY AMBER McMILLAN

The Running Trees
The Woods: A Year on Protection Island
We Can't Ever Do This Again

THIS IS A STICKUP

POEMS

AMBER McMILLAN

A Buckrider Book

© Amber McMillan, 2022

No part of this publication may be reproduced, stored in a retrieval system or transmitted, in any form or by any means, without the prior written consent of the publisher or a license from the Canadian Copyright Licensing Agency (Access Copyright). For an Access Copyright license, visit www.accesscopyright.ca or call toll free to 1-800-893-5777.

Published by Buckrider Books
an imprint of Wolsak and Wynn Publishers
280 James Street North
Hamilton, ON L8R2L3
www.wolsakandwynn.ca

Editor: Paul Vermeersch | Copy editor: Ashley Hisson
Cover and interior design: Jennifer Rawlinson
Cover image: Alisusha/Shutterstock.com
Author photograph: Nathaniel Moore
Typeset in Delicato, Bebas Neue and Mesquite
Printed by Coach House Printing Company, Toronto, Canada

10 9 8 7 6 5 4 3 2 1

The publisher gratefully acknowledges the support of the Ontario Arts Council, the Canada Council for the Arts and the Government of Canada.

Library and Archives Canada Cataloguing in Publication

Title: This is a stickup : poems / Amber McMillan.
Names: McMillan, Amber, 1981- author.
Identifiers: Canadiana 20220285462 | ISBN 9781989496565 (softcover)
Classification: LCC PS8625.M52 T55 2022 | DDC C811/.6—dc23

CONTENTS

PART ONE

This Is a Stickup /3

I Am Earth /4

Another Word for Everything /6

I Have a Recurring Dream /7

Haida Gwaii /8

For You /9

Everything Is Close /10

We Once Traded Poems by Wallace Stevens, Another Thing I Mistook for Love /11

Church on Sunday /12

We're All Afraid of Men /13

The Thing About Deer /14

On the Other Side of an Hour /16

PART TWO

January /19

February /20

March /21

April /22

May /23

June /24

July /25

August /26

September /27

October /28

November /29

December /30

PART THREE

Picture This /33
We're All Afraid of Men II /35
Home for the Holidays /36
The Sisters of Bernini /37
Lunch Break /38
Murder City /39
This Marriage, He Said /41
I Don't Remember Everything, But I Remember This /42
Magician's Contrition /45
We're All Afraid of Men III /46
Newcomer /47
Another Thing About the Atlantic /48

PART FOUR

The Good in You /51
We're All Afraid of Men IV /52
Liver /53
I Am an Orphan /54
We're All Afraid of Men V /55
Lung /56
You're an Orphan Too /57
We're All Afraid of Men VI /60
Stomach /61
Make Your Love a Crown /62
Spleen /63
We're All Afraid of Men VII /64
Heart /65

Acknowledgements /67

PART ONE

THIS IS A STICKUP

For seven nights I dreamt a bevy of pale fish
clawing upstream, their bodies tilting
to the crest, pushing, urgent against the edge

of something out of sight but no less
imminent. The sound of it, frantic, an electric
rumble or a buzzing to set my head on fire.

Chris once said *Work is an act of love*
because it's true, some acts are acts of love
and everything else is not. But he meant

his work, *his* love. He meant fishing the North
Atlantic, cold all day long; he meant silence
and bearing weight, fevers and salt water.

Andy, listen: if I still wrote poems, this one
would be for you because I can't let anything go.
I'm cruel and I'm sorry. I always have been.

I AM EARTH

On the front door I carved
                the image of a wild bear

because I want to create an atmosphere
                of wear and tear.

I lumber here, and this is where I live.
Lumber as in *carry*, as in
                the lumber of our lives.

And I didn't have the kids I didn't have
because you're lying if you say
                we can live in a world

where thirty-six high-schoolers in Calgary
got fucked by their science teacher

and a seventeen-year-old girl
                starved herself to death
because she couldn't bear her childhood,

where babies are tossed in dumpsters
and plastic bags are used for plastic bags
                are used for plastic.

Did you know twenty thousand species
are extinct? That's a number hard to imagine,
a number no different than, say, *billion*;

I know you know the UN says it'll take
thirty to end world hunger –
        thirty billion *a year* –

but did you know the moon rotates
at the same rate it revolves,
meaning the same side
        faces us at all times?

I'm saying if I'm Earth, you're the moon.
If you're water, I'm the electric charge.
        I'm saying the world
    is my oyster.

I'm saying *please* and thinking
    of only one thing.

ANOTHER WORD FOR EVERYTHING

From the flight height of a passing bird,
it must look pitiful, me: mostly doggo by day
except for fitful bursts from the house
to drag garbage to the bins, sort plastic from the tins,
and on an occasion that I've hauled myself awake
and from the dregs of my ordinary agonies,
allowed myself to linger outside with the birds,
endure November's lacing storm or sunlight slip
from a thin row of birch, it must seem
I so rarely have the moxie to go all night, to go
all the way and mean it. *You should know,*
I tell the birds, *a man I love is dying.*
I know, I heard you, I can hear you, they say.

I HAVE A RECURRING DREAM

I'm standing at the source and know everything
is blowing streams of translucent ghosts – powder,
albino bats – forming an arc above the skyline
at its peak, a torrent of particles landing far away
in an unseen, silent pile. There's an outbreak, a squall
of rowdy birds all *hey where you bin* and the workhorse
of my optimism goads me onward. There's a battle.
There's pitiful meaninglessness. There's erosion
and there's a current. I'm holding something small
in the palm of my hand, but the symbolism fails me.
I'm awake but afraid. I'm awake, thankfully,
at the beginning of this decade and think, *You'll
know a sonnet when you see one.* Then *It was love,
it still is, but we have to talk about something else.*

HAIDA GWAII

We'll take summer to visit your mother – here
from the Salish Sea to the Georgia Strait,
then Cape Caution, east through Hecate.

From Moresby to Skidegate, past Sitka spruce,
cedar, shore pine, past yellow cypress and red alder
where the white raven clipped a closed-core

transformer, or east at Sandspit where men
once quit for cannery towns around Kitimaat,
sick to death from smallpox and syphilis.

We are close now to the shivaree: moose milk
and stacked saltines. The blubber of your darkest
dreams. The pell-mell, the fancy-free.

FOR YOU

At your side door
I leaned a persimmon wreath
as a talisman for grief,
     and a history of bad timing.

What remains come spring,
I'll carry in my mind,
     pin it between pricks of light,
and for the whole summer.

EVERYTHING IS CLOSE

My only child skipped ahead
to drag the heel of her boot

through a rain puddle
just as the neighbour's pickup

slid around the corner,
as quiet as a hummingbird

kisses the edge of the edge
of a hollyhock's soft inside.

WE ONCE TRADED POEMS BY WALLACE STEVENS, ANOTHER THING I MISTOOK FOR LOVE

There's a way to know someone
that's as close as a secret, or secretly,
that's as silent as the slip of a wing.

It starts in the middle of the night,
and ends there too, but you have to trace
it all the way back. You had to be

watching from the start, to have already
known it was a circle. By then
it's unspeakable, which is not the same

as a thing unspoken. *Alone*, she said
once, *is when you try to love
a thing unloved, or love no longer,
or love only as you could in a dream.*

CHURCH ON SUNDAY

It's Sunday morning so I guess you're at church.
Maybe you're with your wife, maybe your kids.
Is church a place just for you? Did you go with your ex?
Did you take her after morning's coffee? After sleepy
sex with your eyes closed? Do you hold hands in the pew?
Do you sing along to the hymns, or just mouth the words?
Do you know the words? Do you squeeze her palm
when the spirit reaches you? Do the sermons reach you?
Do the songs? I know, but does it feel like a waterfall
at ten thousand feet? Like ten thousand tiny horses?

WE'RE ALL AFRAID OF MEN

In high school a man, barely a man,
killed his best friend in the world
at a house party, shot him with the gun
he'd been scaring chickens with out back,
shot him because he was drunk, I guess,
because his girlfriend had fallen asleep
on someone else's shoulder, shot him
because he'd already been shooting those chickens
out back and like birds at the break of day,
there we were singing *I'm still here*,
singing *I'm still alive*, singing *lucky me*
because just like that we were living
with all the things we can't live with.

THE THING ABOUT DEER

You said
write a poem
about sex

which I
agreed to do
and which

I wanted
to do
but as I sat

at my desk
and tried
to think hard

tried to get
on the level
all I could

think of
was a joke:
the one

about a hunter
who shoots
a man dead

in the woods
thinking
the man he shot

was a deer,
not because
he *was* a deer,

but because
the man *said*
he was a deer.

ON THE OTHER SIDE OF AN HOUR

Let's say you had known then what you know now:
on the morning you came to visit your friend at home,
even when you knocked on his door, let's say you'd known
when you entered his room that he would already be gone.
Let's say you held a mess of wildflowers in your arms;

you had brought the blooms to improve the atmosphere,
to lay them along his quiet body, and in so doing, draw
communion to him and the slow opening of stained petals
spread along his forearm and stretching to his bare shoulder
where you imagined he would have placed them himself.

Let's say instead of losing, or held at bay as you were,
you had traced the loose map he kept guarded in his mind,
a private reckoning that laced, like stars, *a* to *b* to *c*. Let's say
you had seen it all so clearly it was as if you understood:
the end, the beginning, love, the cockeyed cedar tree.

PART TWO

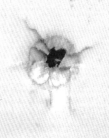

JANUARY

Now that we razed the neighbour's tree
and cut our initials from its brave belly,

now that you're home again, having given up
gluten and porn for good this time,

the view to the outside phone lines is clear:
sparrows were assembling all along.

FEBRUARY

My daughter's best friend
is spending the fourth day in a row

    at our house.
I feed her, I even clothe her,

but she still steals clementines
between meals

    (you won't believe this)
to stave off scurvy.

MARCH

Since you were born, every wish chip or bone,
each streak of light caught in the periphery of a dark sky

is burdened by this prayer for you:
Be happy and good. Stay alive long past me.

APRIL

The truth is you don't know, I say,
the particular kind of trouble I have.

I keep forgetting – I have to remember
that my mind is okay, it's good enough.

What if I can't get better? I wonder.
What if I can't get better? I say.

MAY

Fuck, here we are in the closing
credits and still all this go-go,

still funnelling green toward greener
pastures, still these pass offs

and hand-offs, still punishments
and promises, still *earning* this

and *deserving* that, and whether
we're doomed or not, still the reckless

generosity of translucent clouds
against the sunset, the starlight,

the galactic light, and all I can say
is *wait* and *think of the horses.*

JUNE

My grandfather was born on Father's Day
1926, on the other side of the Atlantic.

He was thirty-three and a father of four
when the tropical depression out of Canaveral

morphed into the storm it became over Miami –
only strengthening through North Carolina –

its warm core blossoming into a hurricane
halfway between Bermuda and New Brunswick.

By landfall it was a cyclone, and by afternoon
it arrived as if from nowhere to tear into the strait

and total all forty-five boats that'd been fishing
for salmon along the coast since morning.

JULY

We are right in the middle
of the meteorological summer,

and I'm thinking to myself,
or I want to, that while my love

for you is an art, I'm still
going to do whatever I want.

AUGUST

Across the country, a man I know
is standing naked in his bedroom

He's left the door open a little
so I can see him if I close my eyes

He's dressing and undressing
to take his daughters to the river

They say it's still possible
to swim in all the rivers out west

SEPTEMBER

Admit a dull shimmer of graphite
carved into a school desk,

cleaved into Formica, reminds
you of a feeling of a feeling.

Goosebumps, maybe, limbs lifting
toward the sun from cool lake water,

licking ribbons of seaweed
below the surface, soft and dark.

Think of a breeze. The buzz of it.

OCTOBER

It's the day of my second marriage
and no one knows but us.

NOVEMBER

That woman described the emptying ghost that follows
her through the murky garden of her sleeping mind.

She runs, she said, and when it's close enough
to touch her, she has just enough time to gasp for air

before its arms are up and through her sternum,
pulling and unfilling her insides to the floor.

She's walking the block in circles – see? – begging
God to spare her just this once, to spare her just tonight.

DECEMBER

I watch the neighbour's guests
cross the street through the snow.

A clumsy party that can't help
but to remind me of another life,

one that lags behind, that sneaks
in a dart before heading inside.

PART THREE

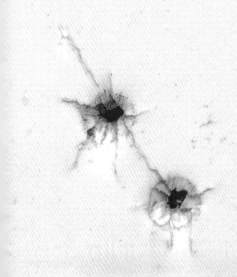

PICTURE THIS

The first time I go fishing, my dad
takes me trolling for trout in Lake Erie.

Maybe you already know the way
sunlight sits on the top layer of water

at 6:30 a.m. near the beginning
of summer, still dark and low below

the surface. You can probably feel
the chill from the night before, too,

the beetling air closest to the lake,
closest to the fish, almost sharp

against your sunburnt skin. There's
Dad, loading his flat of Labatt 50

into his aluminium boat, Ziploc
baggies of this and that, a Thermos

of coffee, say, and maybe Kool-Aid
for me. Too young to fish, I *watch*

and learn, but as soon as we're back
on the dock, picture me losing

focus as Dad shows me just where
to slit their throats, how to pull

the blade back down and through
their soft, prismatic bellies

so the guts fall out in what he called
an organized fashion, picture me

flinch at each jerk of tail, each lurch
of fin, my middle rocking, tossing

til I make what I take as eye contact
with one, let my own roll up my skull,

let the air fill my throat, let the sun-
beams train through my head,

blind me, knock me as slack and quiet
as the fish, its guts abloom around

my untied shoes, my spilled Kool-Aid
slipping pink tentacles into blood.

WE'RE ALL AFRAID OF MEN II

because something isn't clear
                and the bats aren't talking

because this is the true story of my grief

because there was nothing else to do

because I know the truth
                and the truth knows me

because they get everything they want

HOME FOR THE HOLIDAYS

That night you took a problem outside,
past the lobby's telephone booth – remember? –
through the pub doors and onto the sidewalk,
the street lights dragged through their rotation –
green, red, gold – as you knocked the other guy's
teeth in for gawking too long. Out-of-his-mind
stewed, he hit the ground as fast as I've ever seen,
bled a dark puddle around our feet. This wasn't
the first jam you were in, not the first time
you fled the scene, but this time it was Christmas,
so you told the cabbie to turn around, to go back
and check, see if the guy was or wasn't dead.

THE SISTERS OF BERNINI

Where is that smooth educator now
who led us goose-headed fools
through the hoary vaults of Rome?

It was still late in the twentieth century,
before cancer or consequence or karma,
when he gathered us pubescent filles

around the *Ecstasy of Saint Teresa* –
colossal in scale – so we might know
the thrust of God for ourselves.

LUNCH BREAK

I took the long way home
to find three singers and a fiddler,

caps on the ground at their feet.
The breeze finned a passerby's

hair as he joined in the chorus,
his voice thin and pretty.

You could see he'd been to water,
to Redmond's Pond, to bring

back a bloom: bright white,
like cotton in a pint glass of water.

MURDER CITY

In my hometown, women and children
go missing all the time, their bodies
discovered days, sometimes years later.

Where I'm from, eight kids disappeared
in twenty-four months, boys and girls,
on their way to school or a friend's;

the eighth was found in Big Otter Creek
on the tenth concession of South Norwich
Township, naked and bruised, drowned.

The serials get all the attention of course –
the Mad Slasher, the Bedroom Strangler,
the Chambermaid Slayer – but I think

about Georgia Jackson the most,
the twenty-year-old plucked from her car
in 1966 – raped, murdered, smothered –

because the man that admitted to it
lives outside Toronto, and when questioned,
mutters something about truth serum

as he leans in the doorway of a split-level
he shares with his second wife, a blue-
and-white welcome sign hanging just left

of his comb-over. I said, he's living there,
drinking coffee and pissing in the can
of that split-level with his second wife.

THIS MARRIAGE, HE SAID

Each day we mobilize the pink organs
of our home: we sew in rows of blue camas;
like ribbons, we tangle-tie our griefs

to buffalo clover and wild sorrel weeds.
We carry, still, the flames and puzzles
of our former lives in the hidden light

of our separate minds, and each night I come
to you: my canine tongue in one hand –
see – your untroubled love in the other.

I DON'T REMEMBER EVERYTHING, BUT I REMEMBER THIS

Before it burned down, the light from the 'Wick was smaller and lower than any light anywhere else. Light hovering just above the floorboards. All I remember is the grimy pay phone, and every detail of the nights I watched Andy play his guitar from behind a wall of alcohol.

Before it burned down, Dylan made the Embassy his first stop for a pint after another stint at Exeter Road. This last time, while the Embassy was still standing, he'd been inside for 182 days, so I watched him for most of an hour before taking the empty seat on his right to welcome him home. He was different again.

I met Willie Nelson at the London Fair a lightless spring in '97 and under the watchful eyes of his eight bodyguards. They all stood, all but Willie, when I approached the table. Do you know what that's like? Eight guys rising to stand in unison? God, I didn't know what to say. I asked for his signature, so he signed the damp inside of my cigarette pack.

One summer my cousins dragged me outside, held me down and threw earthworms at my head, earthworms they'd been collecting in an empty yogurt container for days. At least some of those worms were already dead before they were hauled out in fistfuls and flung through the air. Before their grey-goo bodies hit my face.

The only time I stayed, the Richmond Hotel had been murder-free since January. There's a floppy calendar tacked up next to the MURDER FREE SINCE sign in the entrance with all twelve months so it's easy to update. I had nowhere better to go, so January was good enough for me.

There's still a top-floor walk-up on Stanley near the Thames, a small and clean place where they brought my mother, just born, back from the hospital in a shoebox. Opa told me the rent was eleven dollars a month in '51. *Good thing I had fourteen*, he said.

My fourth boyfriend drew the image of a black bird I have tattooed on my forearm. One April, I watched him push a needle slowly into the crease of his elbow, the sight of which made me barf right there where I sat. The day we were evicted, we slept in the crawl space between the first and second floors of our building. Tom the Hippie told us the next morning we'd kept him up all night tapping on the floorboards.

When there was nothing to do, and even when there was, the six of us gathered at The Apartment to drink bottomless coffee for a dollar and watch the drag queens get ready for the early show. I had black on the optimistic days, lots of cream and sugar on the lousy ones. Some of those girls were the prettiest girls I'd ever seen.

In '03, a power line in north Ohio brushed a few overgrown trees and shut down, softened from the heat of the current coursing through it. The next hour saw three more sag off, then the rest, tripping a cascade of failures through the Eastern Seaboard. For two days, Keith and I passed each other love notes in the dark and cooked everything we could find on an open fire until his idiot roommate returned home to start a stunt company out of the living room.

Each Christmas they flood Victoria Park in prisms of light. Thousands of strands in hundreds of colours wrapped around every tree there, and for the whole winter. The best view is from atop the Holy Roller stationed as a monument on the west side of the park, one leg on either side of the cannon's barrel.

I spent the summer of '94 in a cave on Dundas. To smoke cigarettes, to make out with Duane, to watch Blockbuster blockbusters. There was a loft above, but you needed a password to get in. To buy dope, to pass out in the hammock, to watch Fred Astaire movies in black and white. It's also where Jeremy hanged himself and Jen spent hours knitting us matching, sea-coloured mittens before going to bed with her adopted father.

I spent the summer of my pregnancy in a dream. I'd already learned how to be alone for days, then weeks, then months at a time. Finn, listen to me, I loved you then and I love you now.

For my first panic attack, Aaron took me to the ER in the belly of a tossed-over shopping cart we found in a late-night shadowed street. I crawled in and Aaron sang only songs I knew the words to as he hauled us both uphill.

For my third or fourth, I gutted a bass amp and crawled inside, hoping to hell no one would see me there. Everything came out: the grate, the tubes, all the delicate filament, the wires, the sharp edges of the whole inside on the floor.

As a child, my hours and days were spent playing hide-and-seek in the backrooms of the family's furniture store. There were paper cones to drink water from and the constancy of wood varnish and sawdust. If I behaved, I could go along with my uncles to get unfinished chairs from the Mennonite farm at the edge of town. Every time except one time, there was ice cream on the way back.

As a child, I learned that boys were better than girls. The details are cloudy, it was their fault or it was your fault, but what I can say with certainty is it was there before I was ten.

On the hottest day of the year, my mum's tipsy friend fired uneven holes through each of my lobes with a plastic gun. She used handfuls of ice from the beer cooler to numb the pain in my ears when it was over.

MAGICIAN'S CONTRITION

For years now,
I have stolen single,
discarded playing cards
from the streets of London.

Cards children collected,
admired and tallied,
then carried to a friend's
in unzippered pockets.

Forgive me,
like in every other way,
in all these fits and starts,
I was trying for a full deck.

WE'RE ALL AFRAID OF MEN III

When I open my eyes
you're at the edge of our bed

and there's already
a baseball bat in your hands.

He's looking right at you,
you hiss, and you're out

of bed, outside and yelling
into the dark of our yard,

at someone at least a block
away by now, someone

who quietly scaled the house
to watch me while I sleep.

NEWCOMER

They say the Atlantic is the youngest,
but the first crossed by ship or plane.

Its surface obscures a mountain range
twice as wide as the Andes, diamonds

in the seabed, the *Titanic*, HMS *Candytuft*
Light Heart, Air France flight four four

seven and *Lord Ashburton*, a merchant
ship from New Brunswick that wrecked

in a nor'easter en route to Saint John.
It's the axis of all weather patterns,

of hurricanes, of the Bermuda Triangle.
The coelacanth fish was extinct for sixty

million years until the live catch of '38
and in this empty room, I know its drift,

its wind against the weakened window
frames. I feel its lift and fall. Its charge.

ANOTHER THING ABOUT THE ATLANTIC

Nova Scotia has been exploding since 1873:
a fire on the jetty of the Bedford Magazine,
gunpowder at Drummond, methane at Westray,
then the '58 bump at Springhill, Cumberland
County, the only pileup of the kind that made
The Ed Sullivan Show, that roused pop songs
and provoked an all-expenses-paid vacation
to Jekyll Island for survivors, a puffery ploy,
it turned out, to draw tourism to Georgia state.

PART FOUR

THE GOOD IN YOU

I'm thinking of the time we walked
all over town collecting booklets
of yellow paper coupons for Coke Zero,
that's Coke without the calories,
but with all the Caramel E150d
we'd ever need to outsmart our bodies.

I'm thinking of the time we walked
all over the AGO, saw the rococos,
the baroques, saw colours, saw worlds –
but none of that counted, no matter what
it provoked, *If I'm standing too close,*
you said, *If I can see the brush strokes.*

WE'RE ALL AFRAID OF MEN IV

The downside is every new beginning, now that I know whenever you return to me, you return to me different.

Let me say this, finally, and to you alone: there is danger at the heart of every living thing, in the heart of it all.

LIVER

The king of Babylon is standing at the parting of the way,
at the head of two ways, to consult his liver, *the seat
of the fire*, he says, *that burns throughout my body.*

He is looking for resentment, but can feel almost nothing
since the dream of stolen fire, of the eagle that came
to lick the sweetness from inside of him, over and over.

I AM AN ORPHAN

I see you there on that island,
overconfident and all alone,
scribbling notes, weighing odds,
burning through *the facts
as you see them*, and unable to
name it, to claim *what went wrong,*
you'll call it *betrayal,* you'll
hide in the pain of others, then
you'll hide in the pain that's yours.

Here's another thing I know:
It's sparrows all the way down,
and everything that can happen,
                happens.

WE'RE ALL AFRAID OF MEN V

My father was always edgy like a teenager is edgy,
drunk, poorly concealing kaleidoscopic turmoil,

frantic mania, the supernatural atmosphere
that intruded into every conversation, every instance

of any thing, the fog of madness lingered, twisted
into smoke, his smoke: he's standing on a table,

a cigarette between loose fingers, spinning a tale.
An old one about a fox and a crow and hunger.

LUNG

You know, the second or so before he died,
Proust told the charcoal figures by his side:

I have just coughed three thousand times,
and then, *There's never any time to write.*

YOU'RE AN ORPHAN TOO

Richard, it's been a year
and everything is different.

You'll be disappointed
to know that I tried,

of course I tried, but I can't
reconcile with my mother.

The situation is worse
than I admitted the summer

we spent stoned under
the apple trees out back

and you asked about
my childhood: *mon petit*

chat noir, you said,
how'd you get so blue?

Before you died, the dog
dug a hole in the yard

to bury his toys. He must've
got hold of your craft box

because come spring,
when the ground softened,

when the snow melted,
when you were gone,

that dirt hole blew open
and pushed out a pinata

of glass beads, yarn,
metallic strips of torn party

decorations you'd saved
from Finn's birthday.

I went across the country
to see the crown of light

around my sister's son,
a child she made with some

out-of-the-picture bro
right before COVID.

In the same doomed town,
I saw an old friend transform

from a bird, or from
a universe disguised as a bird,

into an empty room. I had
no choice but to leave,

Richard, or I *chose* to leave.
And then as soon as I saw

that I could, I left every
other empty room too.

I don't know if I saw you then
or if I saw the night before,

but I see you now. I know
what happened, or I know where

you went in your mind,
where you had to go to do it.

Look, I want you to know
that everything is different,

but it's the cold and quiet end
of another year, just as cold

and quiet as all the ends to all
the years, and I'm still here.

WE'RE ALL AFRAID OF MEN VI

Let's talk about what's good, you say.
Let's talk about what's true.

You're cold and white, I say. *The bright
night of the sun. You're the moon.*

That's the part of me that's sick,
you say. The part of me that's doomed.

STOMACH

A heat-wave field fire
tore through our neighbourhood park
the August you were born.

Wild flames stealed up trees,
rapid and mean, haloing the swing sets,
our abandoned bicycles.

Through the dirty air,
a white van waited at the park's edge
to collect me for the hospital

where Mum was already hollering
herself through another labour –
you this time – and I cried

in the waiting room, trying
to match her pitch, the wailing you out,
the screaming you out of her.

MAKE YOUR LOVE A CROWN
for Nathaniel

I really thought there'd be more records
of the grief I've known all along as private,

grief I've since called *love*, later *madness*,
but which has left me only once since I was born.

SPLEEN

The spleen is purple and beneath the ninth,
tenth and eleventh ribs in every cage.

An easy way to remember is it's vestigial,
the B-list of abdominal machinery,
outshined by all neighbouring organs.

You are no more, Baudelaire warns us all,
than a rock encircled by a nameless dread.
The sun, he goes on, *pours down on us*
a daylight even dingier than the dark.

WE'RE ALL AFRAID OF MEN VII

The first time I heard about love, I eavesdropped
on my brother and his friends in the attic.

One said, *What's the best thing you've ever felt?*
Another, *What's the worst thing you've ever done?*

HEART

A guy sprints down some stairs
and past me into the street – so close

this close to being late for a ten-thirty
court hearing a block away.

He's running fast and he's all alone,
       I'm saying his limbs are swinging,

his shoelaces are flapping – I'm saying
he's wilding down the street on fire.

I think about his heart. No, I don't.
I think about the thousand lonely things

he's done. Then about the thousand
       lonely things I've done.

ACKNOWLEDGEMENTS

Thank you to Noelle, Ashley and Paul at Wolsak & Wynn for your long-term support, expertise and warmth. You really are a dream team.

Thank you to Sue Sinclair for offering your towering mind-heart to many of these poems.

The creation of this book is supported by the New Brunswick Arts Board.

AMBER McMILLAN is the author of the short story collection *The Running Trees* (Goose Lane Editions, 2021), the memoir *The Woods: A Year on Protection Island* (Nightwood Editions, 2016) and the poetry collection *We Can't Ever Do This Again* (Wolsak & Wynn, 2015). Her work has won a Penguin Random House award for fiction and been shortlisted for the Montreal International Poetry Prize, the New Brunswick Book Awards and the Atlantic Book Awards. She lives in New Brunswick on the unceded and unsurrendered territory of the Wolastoqiyik, Mi'kmaq and Peskotomuhkati people.

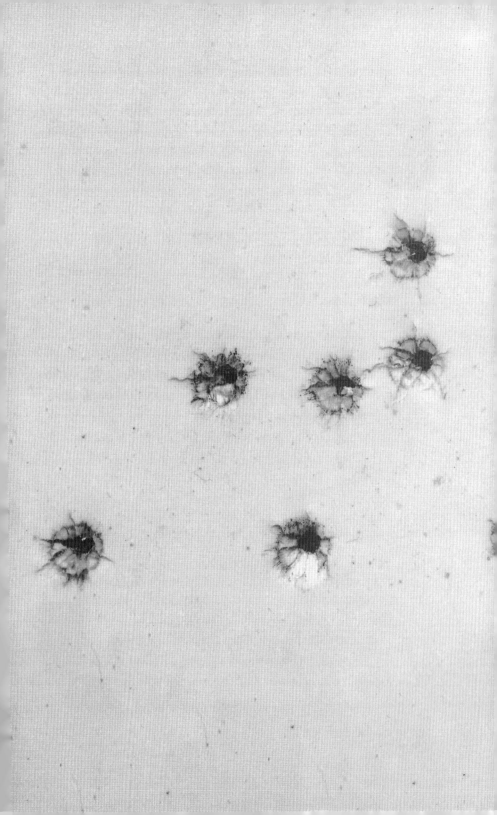

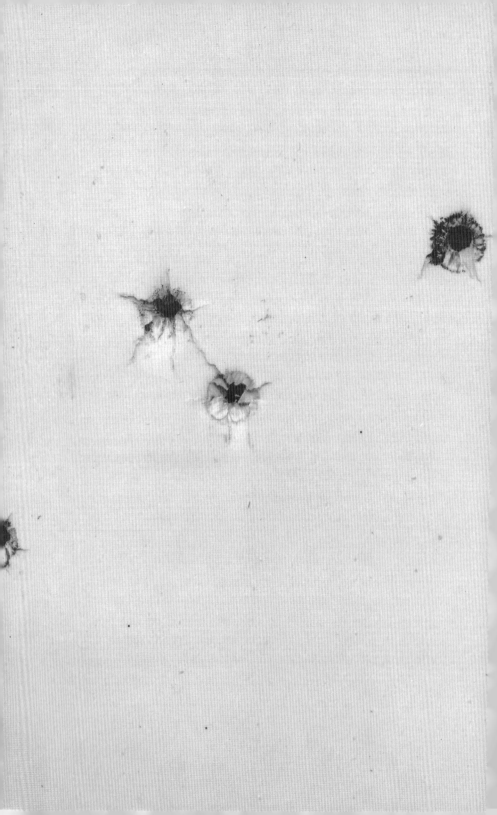